201.6
FRE.82
F

rged for late

2146

THE INTERNATIONAL
PSYCHO-ANALYTICAL
LIBRARY

EDITED BY ERNEST JONES

No. 15

THE INTERNATIONAL PSYCHO-ANALYTICAL LIBRARY
EDITED BY ERNEST JONES
No. 15.

THE FUTURE OF AN ILLUSION

SIGMUND FREUD, M.D., LL.D.

TRANSLATED BY
W. D. ROBSON-SCOTT

THIRD IMPRESSION

PUBLISHED BY THE HOGARTH PRESS,
37, MECKLENBURGH SQUARE, LONDON,
AND THE INSTITUTE OF PSYCHO-ANALYSIS

1943

First published - 1928
Second impression 1934
Third impression - 1943

Printed in Great Britain by
Lowe and Brydone Printers Limited, London, N.W.10

TRANSLATOR'S NOTE

I WISH to express my thanks to the Editor and to Mr. James Strachey for reading through this translation and making many helpful suggestions.

W. D. R.-S.

CHAPTER I

WHEN one has lived for long within a particular culture [1] and has often striven to discover its origins and the path of its development, one feels for once the temptation to turn one's attention in the other direction and to ask what further fate awaits this culture and what transformations it is destined to undergo. But one soon finds that the value of such an enquiry is diminished from the outset by several considerations. Above all, by the fact that there are only a few people who can survey human activity in all its ramifications. Most people have been compelled to restrict themselves to a single, or to a few, spheres of interest ; but the less a man knows of the past and the present the more unreliable must his judgement of the future prove. And further it is precisely in the matter

[1] The German word *Kultur* has been translated sometimes as ' culture ' and sometimes as ' civilization ', denoting as it does a concept intermediate between these and at times inclusive of both.—ED.

of this judgement that the subjective expectations of the individual play a part that is difficult to assess ; for these prove to be dependent on purely personal factors in his own experience, on his more or less hopeful attitude to life, according as temperament, success or failure has prescribed for him.   And finally one must take into account the remarkable fact that in general men experience the present naïvely, so to speak, without being able to estimate its content ; they must first place it at a distance, *i.e.* the present must have become the past before one can win from it points of vantage from which to gauge the future.

And so he who yields to the temptation to deliver an opinion on the probable future of our culture will do well to remind himself of the difficulties just indicated, and likewise of the uncertainty that attaches quite universally to every prophecy.   It follows from this that in hasty flight from so great a task I shall seek out the small tract of territory to which my attention has hitherto been directed, as soon as I have defined its position in general.

Human culture—I mean by that all those respects in which human life has raised itself above animal conditions and in which it differs from the life of the beasts, and I disdain to separate culture and civilization—presents, as is well known, two aspects to the observer. It includes on the one hand all the knowledge and power that men have acquired in order to master the forces of nature and win resources from her for the satisfaction of human needs ; and on the other hand it includes all the necessary arrangements whereby men's relations to each other, and in particular the distribution of the attainable riches, may be regulated. The two tendencies of culture are not independent of each other, first, because the mutual relations of men are profoundly influenced by the measure of instinctual satisfaction that the existing resources make possible; secondly, because the individual can himself take on the quality of a piece of property in his relation to another, in so far as this other makes use of his capacity for work or chooses him as sexual object; and thirdly, because every individual is virtually an enemy of culture, which is nevertheless ostensibly an object of universal human concern. It is remarkable that little as men are able to exist in isolation they should yet feel as a heavy burden the sacrifices that culture expects of them in order that a communal existence may be possible. Thus culture must be defended against the individual, and its organization, its institutions and its laws, are all

directed to this end ; they aim not only at estab-
lishing a certain distribution of property, but also
at maintaining it ; in fact, they must protect
against the hostile impulses of mankind everything
that contributes to the conquest of nature and
the production of wealth. Human creations are
easy to destroy, and science and technical skill,
which have built them up, can also be turned to
their destruction.

So one gets the impression that culture is something which was imposed on a resisting majority
by a minority that understood how to possess
itself of the means of power and coercion. Of
course it stands to reason that these difficulties
are not inherent in the nature of culture itself,
but are conditioned by the imperfections of the
cultural forms that have so far been developed.
Indeed it is not difficult to point out these defects.
While mankind has made solid advances in the
conquest of nature and may expect to make still
greater ones, no certain claim can be established
for a corresponding advance in the regulation
of human affairs, and probably at every period,
as again now, many men have asked themselves
whether this fragment that has been acquired by
culture is indeed worth defending at all. One
might suppose that a reorganization of human

relations should be possible, which, by abandoning coercion and the suppression of the instincts, would remove the sources of dissatisfaction with culture, so that undisturbed by inner conflict men might devote themselves to the acquisition of natural resources and to the enjoyment of the same. That would be the golden age, but it is questionable if such a state of affairs can ever be realized. It seems more probable that every culture must be built up on coercion and instinctual renunciation ; it does not even appear certain that without coercion the majority of human individuals would be ready to submit to the labour necessary for acquiring new means of supporting life. One has, I think, to reckon with the fact that there are present in all men destructive, and therefore anti-social and anti-cultural, tendencies, and that with a great number of people these are strong enough to determine their behaviour in human society.

This psychological fact acquires a decisive significance when one is forming an estimate of human culture. One thought at first that the essence of culture lay in the conquest of nature for the means of supporting life, and in eliminating the dangers that threaten culture by the suitable distribution of these among mankind, but now the emphasis seems to have shifted away from the material plane on to the psychical. The critical question is whether and to what extent one can succeed, first, in diminishing the burden of the instinctual sacrifices imposed on men; secondly, in reconciling them to those that must necessarily remain; and thirdly, in compensating them for these. It is just as impossible to do without government of the masses by a minority as it is to dispense with coercion in the work of civilization, for the masses are lazy and unintelligent, they have no love for instinctual renunciation, they are not to be convinced of its inevitability by argument, and the individuals support each other in giving full play to their unruliness. It is only by the influence of individuals who can set an example, whom the masses recognize as their leaders, that they can be induced to submit to the labours and renunciations on which the existence of culture depends. All is well if these leaders are people of superior insight into what constitute the necessities of life, people who have attained the height of mastering their own instinctual wishes. But the danger exists that in order not to lose their influence they will yield to the masses more than these will yield to them, and therefore it seems necessary that they should be independent of the masses by having at their disposal means of enforcing their authority. To put it briefly, there are two widely diffused human characteristics which are responsible for the fact that the organization of culture can be maintained only by a certain measure of coercion : that is to say, men are not naturally fond of work, and arguments are of no avail against their passions.

I know what objections will be brought against these arguments. It will be said that the character of the masses, here delineated, which is supposed to prove that one cannot dispense with coercion in the work of civilization, is itself only the result of defective cultural organization, through which men have become embittered, revengeful and unapproachable. New generations, brought up kindly and taught to have a respect for reason, who have experienced the benefits of culture early in life, will have a different attitude towards it ; they will feel it to be their very own possession, and they will be ready on its account to make the sacrifice in labour and in instinctual renunciation that is necessary for its preservation. They will be able to do without coercion and will differ little from their leaders. If no culture has so far produced human masses of such a quality, it is due to the fact that no culture has yet discovered the plan that will influence men in such a way, and that from childhood on.

It may be doubted whether it is possible at all, or at any rate just now, in the present stage of our conquest of nature, to establish a cultural organization of this kind ; it may be asked where the throng of superior, dependable and disinterested leaders, who are to act as educators of the future generations, are to come from ; and one may be appalled at the stupendous amount of force that will be unavoidable if these intentions are to be carried out. But one cannot deny the grandeur of this project and its significance for the future of human culture. It is securely based on a piece of psychological insight, on the fact that man is equipped with the most varied instinctual predispositions, the ultimate course of which is determined by the experiences of early childhood. But the limitations of man's capacity for education set bounds to the efficacy of such a cultural transformation. One may question whether and in what degree it would be possible for another cultural milieu to efface the two characteristics of human masses that make the guidance of men's affairs so very difficult. The experiment has not yet been made. Probably a certain percentage of mankind—owing to morbid predisposition or too great instinctual vigour—will always remain asocial, but if only one can succeed in reducing to a minority the majority that is to-day hostile to culture, one will have accomplished a great deal, perhaps indeed everything that can be accomplished.

I should not like to give the impression that I have wandered far away from the chosen path of my enquiry. I will therefore expressly assert that it is far from my intention to estimate the value of the great cultural experiment that is at present in progress in the vast country that stretches between Europe and Asia. I have neither the special knowledge nor the capacity to decide on its practicability, to test the expediency of the methods employed, or to measure the width of the inevitable gulf between intention and execution. What is there in course of preparation eludes investigation, for which it is not ready; for this our long consolidated culture presents the material.

CHAPTER II

WE have glided unawares out of the economic plane over into the psychological. At first we were tempted to seek the essence of culture in the existing material resources and in the arrangements for their distribution. But with the discovery that every culture is based on compulsory labour and instinctual renunciation, and that it therefore inevitably evokes opposition from those affected by these demands, it became clear that the resources themselves, the means of acquiring them, and the arrangements for their distribution could not be its essential or unique characteristic; for they are threatened by the rebelliousness and destructive passions of the members of the culture. Thus in addition to the resources there are the means of defending culture : the coercive measures, and others that are intended to reconcile men to it and to recompense them for their sacrifices. And these last may be described as the psychical sphere of culture.

For the sake of a uniform terminology we will
describe the fact that an instinct cannot be satisfied
as ' frustration ', the means by which this frustration is secured as ' prohibition ', and the condition
produced by the prohibition as ' privation '. Then
the next step is to distinguish between privations
that do affect everybody and those that do not,
those that merely affect groups, classes, or even
individuals. The former are the oldest ; with
the prohibitions that cause them culture began,
who knows how many thousands of years ago, to
detach itself from the primordial animal condition
of mankind. To our surprise we have found that
they are still operative, that they still form the
kernel of the hostility to culture. The instinctual
wishes that suffer under them are born anew with
every child ; there is a class of men, the neurotics,
who react already to this first group of frustra-
tions by an asocial attitude. Such instinctual
wishes are those of incest, of cannibalism, and of
murder. It seems strange to classify these, in
repudiating which all men seem to be at one, with
those others, about whose permissibility or im-
permissibility in our culture there is so vigorous
a dispute ; but psychologically one is justified in
doing this. Nor is the attitude of culture to these
oldest instinctual wishes the same in each case ;

cannibalism alone seems to be proscribed by everyone, and—to other than analytic observation—
completely overcome ; the strength of the incest
wishes can still be perceived behind the prohibition ; and under certain conditions murder is still
practised, indeed enjoined, by our culture. It
is possible that cultural developments lie before us,
in which yet other wish-gratifications, which are
to-day entirely permissible, will appear just as
disagreeable as those of cannibalism do now.

Already in these earliest instinctual renunciations a psychological factor is involved, which
remains of great importance for everything that
follows. It is not true to say that the human
mind has undergone no development since the
earliest times and that in contrast to the advances
of science and technical skill it is still the same to-
day as at the beginning of history. We can point
out one of these advances here. It is in accordance with the course of our development that
external compulsion is gradually internalized, in
that a special mental function, man's super-ego,
takes it under its jurisdiction. Every child presents
to us the model of this transformation ; it is only
by that means that it becomes a moral and social
being. This strengthening of the super-ego is a
highly valuable psychological possession for culture.

Those people in whom it has taken place, from being the foes of culture, become its supporters. The greater their number in a cultural community, the more secure it is and the more easily can it dispense with external coercion. Now the degree of this internalization differs widely in the case of each instinctual prohibition. As far as the earliest demands of culture, already mentioned, are concerned, the process of internalization seems to have been to a great extent accomplished, if we leave out of account the unwelcome exception of the neurotics. But the case is altered when we turn to the other instinctual claims. One notes with surprise and concern that a majority of men obey the cultural prohibitions in question only under the pressure of external force, in fact only where the latter can assert itself and for as long as it is an object of fear. This also holds good for those so-called moral cultural demands, which in the same way apply to everyone. The greater part of what one experiences of man's moral untrustworthiness is to be explained in this connection. There are innumerable civilized people who would shrink from murder or incest, and who yet do not hesitate to gratify their avarice, their aggressiveness and their sexual lusts, and who have no compunction in hurting others by lying, fraud and calumny, so long as they remain unpunished for it ; and no doubt this has been so for many cultural epochs.

If we turn to those restrictions that only apply to certain classes of society, we encounter a state of things which is glaringly obvious and has always been recognized. It is to be expected that the neglected classes will grudge the favoured ones their privileges and that they will do everything in their power to rid themselves of their own surplus of privation. Where this is not possible a lasting measure of discontent will obtain within this culture, and this may lead to dangerous outbreaks. But if a culture has not got beyond the stage in which the satisfaction of one group of its members necessarily involves the suppression of another, perhaps the majority—and this is the case in all modern cultures,—it is intelligible that these suppressed classes should develop an intense hostility to the culture ; a culture, whose existence they make possible by their labour, but in whose resources they have too small a share. In such conditions one must not expect to find an internalization of the cultural prohibitions among the suppressed classes ; indeed they are not even prepared to acknowledge these prohibitions, intent, as they are, on the destruction of the culture itself and perhaps even of the assumptions on which it rests. These classes are so manifestly hostile to culture that on that account the more latent hostility of the better provided social strata has been overlooked. It need not be said that a culture which leaves unsatisfied and drives to rebelliousness so large a number of its members neither has a prospect of continued existence, nor deserves it.

The extent to which cultural rules have been internalized—to express it popularly and un-psychologically : the moral level of the members— is not the only psychical asset to be considered if one is estimating the value of a culture. In addition there is its heritage of ideals and artistic creations, that is to say, of the satisfactions they both yield.

One will be only too readily inclined to include among the psychical possessions of a culture its ideals, that is, its judgements of what are its loftiest and its most ambitious accomplishments. It seems at first as if these ideals would deter-mine the achievements of the cultural group ; but the actual process would seem to be that the ideals are modelled on the first achievements that the co-operation of internal ability and external circumstances made possible, and that now these

B

first achievements are merely held fast by the
ideal as examples to be followed. The satisfaction
the ideal gives to the members of the culture is
thus of a narcissistic nature, it is based on pride
in what has already been successfully achieved.
To make this satisfaction complete the culture
compares itself with others which have applied
themselves to other tasks and have developed
other ideals. On the strength of these differences
every culture claims the right to despise the rest.
In this way cultural ideals become a source of
discord and enmity between different cultural
groups, as can be most clearly seen among nations.

The narcissistic satisfaction provided by the
cultural ideal is also one of the forces that effect-
ively counteract the hostility to culture within
the cultural group. It can be shared not only
by the favoured classes, which enjoy the benefits
of this culture, but also by the suppressed, since
the right to despise those that are outside it
compensates them for the wrongs they suffer in
their own group.   True, one is a miserable plebeian,
tormented by obligations and military service,
but withal one is a Roman citizen, one has one's
share in the task of ruling other nations and
dictating their laws. This identification of the
suppressed with the class that governs and exploits

them is, however, only a part of a larger whole. Thus the former can be attached affectively to the latter ; in spite of their animosity they can find their ideals in their masters. Unless such relations, fundamentally of a satisfying kind, were in existence, it would be impossible to understand how so many cultures have contrived to exist for so long in spite of the justified hostility of great masses of men.

Different in kind is the satisfaction that art yields to the members of a cultural group. As a rule it remains inaccessible to the masses, who are engaged in exhausting labour and who have not enjoyed the benefits of individual education. As we have long known, art offers substitutive gratifications for the oldest cultural renunciations, still always most deeply felt, and for that reason serves like nothing else to reconcile men to the sacrifices they have made on culture's behalf. On the other hand, works of art promote the feelings of identification, of which every cultural group has so much need, in the occasion they provide for the sharing of highly valued emotional experiences. And when they represent the achievements of a particular culture, thus in an impressive way recalling it to its ideals, they also subserve a narcissistic gratification.

No mention has yet been made of what is perhaps the most important part of the psychical inventory of a culture : that is to say, its—in the broadest sense—religious ideas ; in other words, the use of which will be justified later, its illusions.

CHAPTER III

WHEREIN lies the peculiar value of religious ideas ?

We have spoken of the hostility to culture, produced by the pressure it exercises and the instinctual renunciations that it demands. If one imagined its prohibitions removed, then one could choose any woman who took one's fancy as one's sexual object, one could kill without hesitation one's rival or whoever interfered with one in any other way, and one could seize what one wanted of another man's goods without asking his leave : how splendid, what a succession of delights, life would be ! True, one soon finds the first difficulty : everyone else has exactly the same wishes, and will treat one with no more consideration than one will treat him. And so in reality there is only one single person who can be made unrestrictedly happy by abolishing thus the restrictions imposed by culture, and that is a tyrant or dictator who has monopolized all the means of power ; and even he has every reason to want the others to keep at least one cultural commandment : thou shalt not kill.

But how ungrateful, how short-sighted after all, to strive for the abolition of culture ! What would then remain would be the state of nature, and that is far harder to endure. It is true that nature does not ask us to restrain our instincts, she lets us do as we like ; but she has her peculiarly effective mode of restricting us : she destroys us, coldly, cruelly, callously, as it seems to us, and possibly just through what has caused our satisfaction. It was because of these very dangers with which nature threatens us that we united together and created culture, which, amongst other things, is supposed to make our communal existence possible. Indeed, it is the principal task of culture, its real *raison d'être*, to defend us against nature.

One must confess that in many ways it already does this tolerably well, and clearly as time goes on it will be much more successful. But no one is under the illusion that nature has so far been vanquished ; few dare to hope that she will ever be completely under man's subjection. There are the elements, which seem to mock at all human control : the earth, which quakes, is rent asunder, and buries man and all his works ; the water, which in tumult floods and submerges all things ; the storm, which drives all before it ; there are the diseases, which we have only lately recognized as the attacks of other living creatures ; and finally there is the painful riddle of death, for which no remedy at all has yet been found, nor probably ever will be. With these forces nature rises up before us, sublime, pitiless, inexorable ; thus she brings again to mind our weakness and helplessness, of which we thought the work of civilization had rid us. It is one of the few noble and gratifying spectacles that men can offer, when in the face of an elemental catastrophe they awake from their muddle and confusion, forget all their internal difficulties and animosities, and remember the great common task, the preservation of mankind against the supremacy of nature.

For the individual, as for mankind in general, life is hard to endure. The culture in which he shares imposes on him some measure of privation, and other men occasion him a certain degree of suffering, either in spite of the laws of this culture or because of its imperfections. Add to this the evils that unvanquished nature—he calls it Fate —inflicts on him. One would expect a permanent condition of anxious suspense and a severe injury

to his innate narcissism to be the result of this state
of affairs. We know already how the individual
reacts to the injuries that culture and other men
inflict on him : he develops a corresponding degree
of resistance against the institutions of this culture,
of hostility towards it. But how does he defend
himself against the supremacy of nature, of fate,
which threatens him, as it threatens all ?

Culture relieves him of this task : it performs
it in the same way for everyone. (It is also
noteworthy that pretty well all cultures are the
same in this respect.) It does not cry a halt, as
it were, in its task of defending man against
nature ; it merely pursues it by other methods.
This is a complex business ; man's seriously
menaced self-esteem craves for consolation, life
and the universe must be rid of their terrors, and
incidentally man's curiosity, reinforced, it is true,
by the strongest practical motives, demands an
answer.

With the first step, which is the humanization
of nature, much is already won. Nothing can be
made of impersonal forces and fates ; they remain
eternally remote. But if the elements have passions that rage like those in our own souls, if death
itself is not something spontaneous, but the violent
act of an evil Will, if everywhere in nature we

have about us beings who resemble those of our own environment, then indeed we can breathe freely, we can feel at home in face of the supernatural, and we can deal psychically with our frantic anxiety. We are perhaps still defenceless, but no longer helplessly paralysed; we can at least react; perhaps indeed we are not even defenceless, we can have recourse to the same methods against these violent supermen of the beyond that we make use of in our own community; we can try to exorcise them, to appease them, to bribe them, and so rob them of part of their power by thus influencing them. Such a substitution of psychology for natural science provides not merely immediate relief, it also points the way to a further mastery of the situation.

For there is nothing new in this situation. It has an infantile prototype, and is really only the continuation of this. For once before one has been in such a state of helplessness: as a little child in one's relationship to one's parents. For one had reason to fear them, especially the father, though at the same time one was sure of his protection against the dangers then known to one. And so it was natural to assimilate and combine the two situations. Here, too, as in dream-life, the wish came into its own. The sleeper is seized

by a presentiment of death, which seeks to carry
him to the grave. But the dream-work knows
how to select a condition that will turn even this
dreaded event into a wish-fulfilment : the dreamer
sees himself in an ancient Etruscan grave, into
which he has descended, happy in the satisfaction
it has given to his archæological interests. Simi-
larly man makes the forces of nature not simply
in the image of men with whom he can associate
as his equals—that would not do justice to the
overpowering impression they make on him—but
he gives them the characteristics of the father,
makes them into gods, thereby following not only
an infantile, but also, as I have tried to show, a
phylogenetic prototype.

In the course of time the first observations of
law and order in natural phenomena are made,
and therewith the forces of nature lose their
human traits. But men's helplessness remains,
and with it their father-longing and the gods.
The gods retain their threefold task : they must
exorcise the terrors of nature, they must reconcile
one to the cruelty of fate, particularly as shown
in death, and they must make amends for the
sufferings and privations that the communal life
of culture has imposed on man.

But within these there is a gradual shifting of

the accent. It is observed that natural phenomena develop of themselves from inward necessity; without doubt the gods are the lords of nature : they have arranged it thus and now they can leave it to itself. Only occasionally, in the so-called miracles, do they intervene in its course, as if to protest that they have surrendered nothing of their original sphere of power. As far as the vicissitudes of fate are concerned, an unpleasant suspicion persists that the perplexity and help-lessness of the human race cannot be remedied. This is where the gods are most apt to fail us ; if they themselves make fate, then their ways must be deemed inscrutable. The most gifted people of the ancient world dimly surmised that above the gods stands Destiny and that the gods them-selves have their destinies. And the more auto-nomous nature becomes and the more the gods withdraw from her, the more earnestly are all expectations concentrated on the third task as-signed to them and the more does morality become their real domain. It now becomes the business of the gods to adjust the defects and evils of culture, to attend to the sufferings that men inflict on each other in their communal life, and to see that the laws of culture, which men obey so ill, are carried out. The laws of culture themselves are claimed to be of divine origin, they are elevated to a position above human society, and they are extended over nature and the universe.

And so a rich store of ideas is formed, born of the need to make tolerable the helplessness of man, and built out of the material offered by memories of the helplessness of his own childhood and the childhood of the human race. It is easy to see that these ideas protect man in two directions; against the dangers of nature and fate, and against the evils of human society itself. What it amounts to is this: life in this world serves a higher purpose; true, it is not easy to guess the nature of this purpose, but certainly a perfecting of human existence is implied. Probably the spiritual part of man, the soul, which in the course of time has so slowly and unwillingly detached itself from the body, is to be regarded as the object of this elevation and exaltation. Everything that takes place in this world expresses the intentions of an Intelligence, superior to us, which in the end, though its devious ways may be difficult to follow, orders everything for good, that is, to our advantage. Over each one of us watches a benevolent, and only apparently severe, Providence, which will not suffer us to become the plaything of the stark and pitiless forces of nature;

death itself is not annihilation, not a return to inorganic lifelessness, but the beginning of a new kind of existence, which lies on the road of development to something higher. And to turn to the other side of the question, the moral laws that have formed our culture govern also the whole universe, only they are upheld with incomparably more force and consistency by a supreme judicial court. In the end all good is rewarded, all evil punished, if not actually in this life, then in the further existences that begin after death. And thus all the terrors, the sufferings, and the hardships of life are destined to be obliterated ; the life after death, which continues our earthly existence as the invisible part of the spectrum adjoins the visible, brings all the perfection that perhaps we have missed here. And the superior wisdom that directs this issue, the supreme goodness that expresses itself thus, the justice that thus achieves its aim—these are the qualities of the divine beings who have fashioned us and the world in general ; or rather of the one divine being into which in our culture all the gods of antiquity have been condensed. The race that first succeeded in thus concentrating the divine qualities was not a little proud of this advance. It had revealed the father nucleus which had always lain hidden behind every divine figure ; fundamentally it was a return to the historical beginnings of the idea of God. Now that God was a single person, man's relations to him could recover the intimacy and intensity of the child's relation to the father. If one had done so much for the father, then surely one would be rewarded —at least the only beloved child, the chosen people, would be. More recently, pious America has laid claim to be ' God's own country ', and for one of the forms under which men worship the deity the claim certainly holds good.

The religious ideas that have just been summarized have of course gone through a long process of development, and have been held in various phases by various cultures. I have singled out one such phase of development, which more or less corresponds to the final form of our contemporary Christian culture in the west. It is easy to see that not all the parts of this whole tally equally well with each other, that not all the questions that press for an answer receive one, and that the contradiction of daily experience can only with difficulty be dismissed. But such as they are, these ideas—religious, in the broadest sense of the word—are prized as the most precious possession of culture, as the most valuable thing

it has to offer its members ; far more highly
prized than all our devices for winning the treasures
of the earth, for providing men with sustenance,
or for preventing their diseases, and so forth ;
men suppose that life would be intolerable if they
did not accord these ideas the value that is claimed
for them. And now the question arises : what
are these ideas in the light of psychology ; whence
do they derive the esteem in which they are held ;
and further, in all diffidence, what is their real
worth ?

CHAPTER IV

AN enquiry that proceeds uninterruptedly, like a monologue, is not altogether without its dangers. One is too easily tempted to push aside thoughts that would interrupt it, and in exchange one is left with a feeling of uncertainty which one will drown in the end by over-decisiveness. I shall therefore imagine an opponent who follows my arguments with mistrust, and I shall let him interject remarks here and there.

I hear him saying : ' You have repeatedly used the expressions " culture creates these religious ideas ", " culture places them at the disposal of its members ", which sounds strange to me somehow. I could not say why myself, but it does not sound so natural as to say that culture has made regulations about distributing the products of labour or about the rights over women and children.'

I think, nevertheless, that one is justified in expressing oneself thus. I have tried to show that religious ideas have sprung from the same need

as all the other achievements of culture : from the
necessity for defending itself against the crushing
supremacy of nature. And there was a second
motive : the eager desire to correct the so pain-
fully felt imperfections of culture. Moreover,
there is something particularly apposite in saying
that culture gives the individual these ideas, for
he finds them at hand, they are presented to him
ready-made ; he would not be in a position to
find them by himself. It is the heritage of many
generations which he enters into and which he
takes over as he does the multiplication table,
geometry, etc. There is certainly a distinction in
this, but it lies elsewhere, and I cannot examine it
at this point. The feeling of strangeness that you
mention may be partly accounted for by the fact
that this stock of religious ideas is generally offered
as a divine revelation. But that is in itself a part
of the religious system, and entirely leaves out of
account the known historical development of these
ideas and their variations in different ages and
cultures.

' Another point which seems to me more
important. You would derive the humanization
of nature from the desire to put an end to human
perplexity and helplessness in the face of nature's
dreaded forces, and from the necessity for estab-

C

lishing relations with, and finally influencing, these forces. But this explanation seems to be superfluous. For primitive man has no choice, he has no other way of thinking. It is natural to him, as if innate, to project his existence outwards into the world, and to regard all events that come under his observation as the manifestations of beings who fundamentally resemble himself. It is his only method of comprehension. And it is by no means self-evident, on the contrary it is a remarkable coincidence, that he should succeed in satisfying one of his great wants by thus indulging his natural disposition.'

I do not find that so striking. For do you suppose that men's thought-processes have no practical motives, that they are simply the expression of a disinterested curiosity ? That is surely very improbable. I believe, rather, that when he personifies the forces of nature man is once again following an infantile prototype. He has learnt from the persons of his earliest environment that the way to influence them is to establish a relationship with them, and so, later on, with the same end in view, he deals with everything that happens to him as he dealt with those persons. Thus I do not contradict your descriptive observation ; it is, in point of fact, natural to man to personify

everything that he wishes to comprehend, in order
that later he may control it—the psychical sub-
jugation as preparation for the physical—but I
provide in addition a motive and genesis for this
peculiarity of human thought.

' And now yet a third point. You have dealt
with the origin of religion once before, in your book
Totem und Tabu. But there it appears in a
different light. Everything is the son-father relationship ; God is the exalted father, and the
longing for the father is the root of the need for
religion. Since then, it seems, you have discovered
the factor of human weakness and helplessness,
to which indeed the chief part in the formation
of religion is commonly assigned, and you now
transfer to helplessness everything that was
formerly father complex. May I ask you to
enlighten me on this transformation ? '

With pleasure. I was only waiting for this
invitation. But is it really a transformation ?
In *Totem und Tabu* it was not my purpose to
explain the origin of religions, but only of totemism.
Can you from any standpoint known to you explain
the fact that the first form in which the protecting
deity revealed itself to men was that of an animal,
that a prohibition existed against killing or eating
this animal, and that yet it was the solemn custom

to kill it and eat it communally once a year ? It
is just this that takes place in totemism. And
it is hardly to the purpose to argue whether
totemism should be called a religion. It has
intimate connections with the later god-religions ;
the totem animals become the sacred animals of
the gods ; and the earliest, and the most profound,
moral restrictions—the murder prohibition and
the incest prohibition—originate in totemism.
Whether or not you accept the conclusions of
Totem und Tabu, I hope you will admit that in
that book a number of very remarkable isolated
facts are brought together into a consistent whole.

Why in the long run the animal god did not
suffice and why it was replaced by the human—
that was hardly discussed in *Totem und Tabu,*
and other problems of the formation of religion
find no mention there at all. But do you regard
such a limitation as identical with a denial ? My
work is a good example of the strict isolation of
the share that psycho-analytic observation can
contribute to the problem of religion. If I am
now trying to add to it the other, less deeply
hidden, part, you should not accuse me of inconsistency, just as before I was accused of being
one-sided. It is of course my business to point
out the connecting links between what I said

before and what I now put forward, between the
deeper and the manifest motivation, between the
father complex and man's helplessness and need
for protection.

These connections are not difficult to find.
They consist in the relation of the child's helplessness to the adult's continuation of it, so that, as
was to be expected, the psycho-analytic motivation of the forming of religion turns out to be the
infantile contribution to its manifest motivation.
Let us imagine to ourselves the mental life of
the small child.   You remember the object-choice
after the anaclitic type, which psycho-analysis
talks about ?   The libido follows the paths of
narcissistic needs, and attaches itself to the objects
that ensure their satisfaction.   So the mother,
who satisfies hunger, becomes the first love-object,
and certainly also the first protection against all
the undefined and threatening dangers of the outer
world ; becomes, if we may so express it, the first
protection against anxiety.

In this function the mother is soon replaced
by the stronger father, and this situation persists
from now on over the whole of childhood.   But
the relation to the father is affected by a peculiar
ambivalence.   He was himself a danger, perhaps
just because of that earlier relation to the mother ;

so he is feared no less than he is longed for and admired. The indications of this ambivalence are deeply imprinted in all religions, as is brought out in *Totem und Tabu*. Now when the child grows up and finds that he is destined to remain a child for ever, and that he can never do without protection against unknown and mighty powers, he invests these with the traits of the father-figure ; he creates for himself the gods, of whom he is afraid, whom he seeks to propitiate, and to whom he nevertheless entrusts the task of protecting him. Thus the longing-for-the-father explanation is identical with the other, the need for protection against the consequences of human weakness ; the child's defensive reaction to his helplessness gives the characteristic features to the adult's reaction to his own sense of helplessness, *i.e.* the formation of religion. But it is not our intention to pursue further the development of the idea of God ; we are concerned here with the matured stock of religious ideas as culture transmits them to the individual.

CHAPTER V

Now to take up again the threads of our enquiry : what is the psychological significance of religious ideas and how can we classify them ? The question is at first not at all easy to answer. Having rejected various formulas, I shall take my stand by this one : religion consists of certain dogmas, assertions about facts and conditions of external (or internal) reality, which tell one something that one has not oneself discovered and which claim that one should give them credence. As they give information about what are to us the most interesting and important things in life, they are particularly highly valued. He who knows nothing of them is ignorant indeed, and he who has assimilated them may consider himself enriched.

There are of course many such dogmas about the most diverse things of this world. Every school hour is full of them. Let us choose geography. We hear there: Konstanz is on the Bodensee. A student song adds: If you don't believe it go and see. I happen to have been there, and can confirm the fact that this beautiful town lies on the shore of a broad stretch of water, which all those dwelling around call the Bodensee. I am now completely convinced of the accuracy of this geographical statement. And in this connection I am reminded of another and very remarkable experience. I was already a man of mature years when I stood for the first time on the hill of the Athenian Acropolis, between the temple ruins, looking out on to the blue sea. A feeling of astonishment mingled with my pleasure, which prompted me to say: then it really is true, what we used to be taught at school! How shallow and weak at that age must have been my belief in the real truth of what I heard if I can be so astonished to-day! But I will not emphasize the significance of this experience too much; yet another explanation of my astonishment is possible, which did not strike me at the time, and which is of a wholly subjective nature and connected with the peculiar character of the place.

All such dogmas as these, then, exact belief in their contents, but not without substantiating their title to this. They claim to be the condensed result of a long process of thought, which is founded on observation and also, certainly, on reasoning ; they show how, if one so intends, one can go through this process oneself, instead of accepting the result of it ; and the source of the knowledge imparted by the dogma is always added, where it is not, as with geographical statements, self-evident. For instance : the earth is shaped like a globe ; the proofs adduced for this are Foucault's pendulum experiment, the phenomena of the horizon and the possibility of circumnavigating the earth. Since it is impracticable, as all concerned realize, to send every school child on a voyage round the world, one is content that the school teaching shall be taken on trust, but one knows that the way to personal conviction is still open.

Let us try to apply the same tests to the dogmas of religion. If we ask on what their claim to be believed is based, we receive three answers, which accord remarkably ill with one another. They deserve to be believed : firstly, because our primal ancestors already believed them ; secondly, because we possess proofs, which have been handed down to us from this very period of antiquity ; and thirdly, because it is forbidden to raise the question of their authenticity at all. Formerly this presumptuous act was visited with the very severest penalties, and even to-day society is unwilling to see anyone renew it.

This third point cannot but rouse our strongest suspicions. Such a prohibition can surely have only one motive : that society knows very well the uncertain basis of the claim it makes for its religious doctrines. If it were otherwise, the relevant material would certainly be placed most readily at the disposal of anyone who wished to gain conviction for himself. And so we proceed to test the other two arguments with a feeling of mistrust not easily allayed. We ought to believe because our forefathers believed. But these ancestors of ours were far more ignorant than we ; they believed in things we could not possibly accept to-day ; so the possibility occurs that religious doctrines may also be in this category. The proofs they have bequeathed to us are deposited in writings that themselves bear every trace of being untrustworthy. They are full of contradictions, revisions, and interpolations; where they speak of actual authentic proofs they are themselves of doubtful authenticity. It does not help much if divine revelation is asserted to be the origin of their text or only of their content, for this assertion is itself already a part of those doctrines whose authenticity is to be examined, and no statement can bear its own proof.

Thus we arrive at the singular conclusion that just what might be of the greatest significance for us in our cultural system, the information which should solve for us the riddles of the universe and reconcile us to the troubles of life, that just this has the weakest possible claim to authenticity. We should not be able to bring ourselves to accept anything of as little concern to us as the fact that whales bear young instead of laying eggs, if it were not capable of better proof than this.

This state of things is in itself a very remarkable psychological problem. Let no one think that the foregoing remarks on the impossibility of proving religious doctrines contain anything new. It has been felt at all times, assuredly even by the ancestors who bequeathed this legacy. Probably many of them nursed the same doubts as we, but the pressure imposed on them was too strong for them to have dared to utter them. And since then countless people have been tortured by the same doubts, which they would fain have suppressed because they held themselves in duty bound to believe, and since then many brilliant intellects have been wrecked upon this conflict and many characters have come to grief through the compromises by which they sought a way out.

If all the arguments that are put forward for the authenticity of religious doctrines originate in the past, it is natural to look round and see whether the present, better able to judge in these matters, cannot also furnish such evidence. The whole of the religious system would become infinitely more credible if one could succeed in this way in removing the element of doubt from a single part of it. It is at this point that the activity of the spiritualists comes in ; they are convinced of the immortality of the individual soul, and they would demonstrate to us that this one article of religious teaching is free from doubt. Unfortunately they have not succeeded in disproving the fact that the appearances and utterances of their spirits are merely the productions of their own mental activity. They have called up the spirits of the greatest of men, of the most eminent thinkers, but all their utterances and all the information they have received from them have been so foolish and so desperately insignificant that one could find nothing else to believe in but the capacity of the spirits for adapting themselves to the circle of people that had evoked them.

One must now mention two attempts to evade the problem, which both convey the impression of frantic effort. One of them, high-handed in its nature, is old; the other is subtle and modern. The first is the *Credo quia absurdum* of the early Father. It would imply that religious doctrines are outside reason's jurisdiction; they stand above reason. Their truth must be inwardly felt : one does not need to comprehend them. But this *Credo* is only of interest as a voluntary confession ; as a decree it has no binding force. Am I to be obliged to believe every absurdity ? And if not, why just this one ? There is no appeal beyond reason. And if the truth of religious doctrines is dependent on an inner experience which bears witness to that truth, what is one to make of the many people who do not have that rare experience ? One may expect all men to use the gift of reason that they possess, but one cannot set up an obligation that shall apply to all on a basis that only exists for quite a few. Of what significance is it for other people that you have won from a state of ecstasy, which has deeply moved you, an imperturbable conviction of the real truth of the doctrines of religion ?

The second attempt is that of the philosophy of 'As If'. It explains that in our mental activity

we assume all manner of things, the groundless-
ness, indeed the absurdity, of which we fully
realize. They are called 'fictions', but from a
variety of practical motives we are led to behave
'as if' we believed in these fictions. This, it is
argued, is the case with religious doctrines on
account of their unequalled importance for the
maintenance of human society.[1] This argument is
not far removed from the *Credo quia absurdum*.
But I think that the claim of the philosophy of
'As If' is such as only a philosopher could make.
The man whose thinking is not influenced by the
wiles of philosophy will never be able to accept
it ; with the confession of absurdity, of illogicality,
there is no more to be said as far as he is concerned. He cannot be expected to forgo the
guarantees he demands for all his usual activities
just in the matter of his most important interests.
I am reminded of one of my children who was
distinguished at an early age by a peculiarly

---

[1] I hope I am not doing an injustice if I make the author of
the philosophy of ' As If ' represent a point of view that is familiar
to other thinkers also. Cp. H. Vaihinger, *Die Philosophie des Als
ob*, Siebente und achte Auflage, 1922, S. 68 : ' We include as
fictions not merely indifferent theoretical operations but ideational
constructions emanating from the noblest minds, to which the
noblest part of mankind cling and of which they will not allow
themselves to be deprived. Nor is it our object so to deprive
them—for as *practical fictions* we leave them all intact ; they
perish only as *theoretical truths*' (C. K. Ogden's translation).

marked sense of reality. When the children were told a fairy tale, to which they listened with rapt attention, he would come forward and ask : Is that a true story ? Having been told that it was not, he would turn away with an air of disdain. It is to be expected that men will soon behave in like manner towards the religious fairy tales, despite the advocacy of the philosophy of 'As If'.

But at present they still behave quite differently, and in past ages, in spite of their incontrovertible lack of authenticity, religious ideas have exercised the very strongest influence on mankind. This is a fresh psychological problem. We must ask where the inherent strength of these doctrines lies and to what circumstance they owe their efficacy, independent, as it is, of the acknowledgement of the reason.

CHAPTER VI

I THINK we have sufficiently paved the way for the answer to both these questions. It will be found if we fix our attention on the psychical origin of religious ideas. These, which profess to be dogmas, are not the residue of experience or the final result of reflection ; they are illusions, fulfilments of the oldest, strongest and most insistent wishes of mankind ; the secret of their strength is the strength of these wishes. We know already that the terrifying effect of infantile helplessness aroused the need for protection—protection through love—which the father relieved, and that the discovery that this helplessness would continue through the whole of life made it necessary to cling to the existence of a father—but this time a more powerful one. Thus the benevolent rule of divine providence allays our anxiety in face of life's dangers, the establishment of a moral world order ensures the fulfilment of the demands of justice, which within human culture have so often remained unfulfilled, and the prolongation of earthly existence by a future life provides in addition the local and temporal setting for these wish-fulfilments. Answers to the questions that tempt human curiosity, such as the origin of the universe and the relation between the body and the soul, are developed in accordance with the underlying assumptions of this system; it betokens a tremendous relief for the individual psyche if it is released from the conflicts of childhood arising out of the father complex, which are never wholly overcome, and if these conflicts are afforded a universally accepted solution.

When I say that they are illusions, I must define the meaning of the word. An illusion is not the same as an error, it is indeed not necessarily an error. Aristotle's belief that vermin are evolved out of dung, to which ignorant people still cling, was an error; so was the belief of a former generation of doctors that *tabes dorsalis* was the result of sexual excess. It would be improper to call these errors illusions. On the other hand, it was an illusion on the part of Columbus that he had discovered a new sea-route to India. The part played by his wish in this error is very clear. One may describe as an illusion the statement of certain nationalists that the Indo-Germanic race

D

is the only one capable of culture, or the belief, which only psycho-analysis destroyed, that the child is a being without sexuality. It is characteristic of the illusion that it is derived from men's wishes ; in this respect it approaches the psychiatric delusion, but it is to be distinguished from this, quite apart from the more complicated structure of the latter. In the delusion we emphasize as essential the conflict with reality ; the illusion need not be necessarily false, that is to say, unrealizable or incompatible with reality. For instance, a poor girl may have an illusion that a prince will come and fetch her home. It is possible ; some such cases have occurred. That the Messiah will come and found a golden age is much less probable ; according to one's personal attitude one will classify this belief as an illusion or as analogous to a delusion. Examples of illusions that have come true are not easy to discover, but the illusion of the alchemists that all metals can be turned into gold may prove to be one. The desire to have lots of gold, as much gold as possible, has been considerably damped by our modern insight into the nature of wealth, yet chemistry no longer considers a transmutation of metals into gold as impossible. Thus we call a belief an illusion when wish-fulfilment is a prominent factor in its motivation, while disregarding its relations to reality, just as the illusion itself does.

If after this survey we turn again to religious doctrines, we may reiterate that they are all illusions, they do not admit of proof, and no one can be compelled to consider them as true or to believe in them. Some of them are so improbable, so very incompatible with everything we have laboriously discovered about the reality of the world, that we may compare them—taking adequately into account the psychological differences—to delusions. Of the reality value of most of them we cannot judge; just as they cannot be proved, neither can they be refuted. We still know too little to approach them critically. The riddles of the universe only reveal themselves slowly to our enquiry, to many questions science can as yet give no answer; but scientific work is our only way to the knowledge of external reality. Again, it is merely illusion to expect anything from intuition or trance; they can give us nothing but particulars, which are difficult to interpret, about our own mental life, never information about the questions that are so lightly answered by the doctrines of religion. It would be wanton to let one's own arbitrary action fill the gap, and according to one's personal estimate declare this or that part of the religious system to be more or less acceptable. These questions are too momentous for that; too sacred, one might say.

At this point it may be objected : well, then, if even the crabbed sceptics admit that the statements of religion cannot be confuted by reason, why should not I believe in them, since they have so much on their side—tradition, the concurrence of mankind, and all the consolation they yield ? Yes, why not ? Just as no one can be forced into belief, so no one can be forced into unbelief. But do not deceive yourself into thinking that with such arguments you are following the path of correct reasoning. If ever there was a case of facile argument, this is one. Ignorance is ignorance; no right to believe anything is derived from it. No reasonable man will behave so frivolously in other matters or rest content with such feeble grounds for his opinions or for the attitude he adopts; it is only in the highest and holiest things that he allows this. In reality these are only attempts to delude oneself or other people into the belief that one still holds fast to religion, when one has long cut oneself loose from it. Where questions of religion are concerned people are guilty of every possible kind of insincerity and intellectual misdemeanour. Philosophers stretch the meaning of words until they retain scarcely anything of their original sense ; by calling ' God ' some vague abstraction which they have created for themselves, they pose as deists, as believers, before the world ; they may even pride themselves on having attained a higher and purer idea of God, although their God is nothing but an insubstantial shadow and no longer the mighty personality of religious doctrine. Critics persist in calling ' deeply religious ' a person who confesses to a sense of man's insignificance and impotence in face of the universe, although it is not this feeling that constitutes the essence of religious emotion, but rather the next step, the reaction to it, which seeks a remedy against this feeling. He who goes no further, he who humbly acquiesces in the insignificant part man plays in the universe, is, on the contrary, irreligious in the truest sense of the word.

It does not lie within the scope of this enquiry to estimate the value of religious doctrines as truth. It suffices that we have recognized them, psychologically considered, as illusions. But we need not conceal the fact that this discovery strongly influences our attitude to what must appear to many the most important of questions.

We know approximately at what periods and by
what sort of men religious doctrines were formed.
If we now learn from what motives this happened,
our attitude to the problem of religion will suffer
an appreciable change. We say to ourselves : it
would indeed be very nice if there were a God,
who was both creator of the world and a benevolent providence, if there were a moral world order
and a future life, but at the same time it is very
odd that this is all just as we should wish it
ourselves. And it would be still odder if our
poor, ignorant, enslaved ancestors had succeeded
in solving all these difficult riddles of the universe.

CHAPTER VII

HAVING recognized religious doctrines to be illusions, we are at once confronted with the further question : may not other cultural possessions, which we esteem highly and by which we let our life be ruled, be of a similar nature ? Should not the assumptions that regulate our political institutions likewise be called illusions, and is it not the case that in our culture the relations between the sexes are disturbed by an erotic illusion, or by a series of erotic illusions ? Once our suspicions have been roused, we shall not shrink from asking whether there is any better foundation for our conviction that it is possible to discover something about external reality through the applying of observation and reasoning in scientific work. Nothing need keep us from applying observation to our own natures or submitting the process of reasoning to its own criticism. Here a series of enquiries present themselves, which in their result should be of decisive importance for construct-

ing a 'Weltanschauung'. We surmise, too, that
such an endeavour would not be wasted, and that
it would at least partially justify our suspicions.
But the author of these pages has not the means
to undertake so comprehensive a task ; forced by
necessity, he confines his work to the pursuit of
a single one of these illusions, that is, the religious.

But now the loud voice of our opponent bids
us to stop. We are called to account for our
transgressions.

' Archæological interests are no doubt most
praiseworthy, but one does not set about an
excavation if one is thereby going to undermine
occupied dwelling-places so that they collapse and
bury the inhabitants under their ruins. The
doctrines of religion are not a subject that one
can be clever about, as one can about any other.
Our culture is built up on them ; the preservation
of human society rests on the assumption that
the majority of mankind believe in the truth of
these doctrines. If they are taught that there
is no almighty and all just God, no divine world
order, and no future life, then they will feel exempt
from all obligation to follow the rules of culture.
Uninhibited and free from fear, everybody will
follow his asocial, egoistic instincts, and will seek
to prove his power. Chaos, which we have

banished through thousands of years of the work
of civilization, will begin again. Even if one
knew, and could prove, that religion was not in
possession of the truth, one should conceal the
fact and behave as the philosophy of "As If"
demands—and this in the interests of the preservation of everybody. And apart from the danger
of the undertaking, it is also a purposeless cruelty.
Countless people find their one consolation in the
doctrines of religion, and only with their help can
they endure life. You would rob them of what
supports them, and yet you have nothing better
to give them in exchange. It has been admitted
that so far science has not achieved much, but
even if it had advanced far further, it would not
suffice for men. Man has yet other imperative
needs, which can never be satisfied by cold science,
and it is very strange—to be frank, it is the acme
of inconsistency—that a psychologist who has
always emphasized how much in men's lives the
intelligence retreats before the life of the instincts
should now strive to rob men of a precious wish-
satisfaction, and should want to give them in
exchange a compensation of an intellectual nature.'

What a number of accusations all at once!
However, I am prepared to deny them all; and
what is more, I am prepared to defend the state-

ment that culture incurs a greater danger by maintaining its present attitude to religion than by relinquishing it. But I hardly know where to begin my reply.

Perhaps with the assurance that I myself consider my undertaking to be completely harmless and free from danger. This time the over-estimation of the intellect is not on my side. If men are such as my opponents describe them— and I have no wish to contradict it—then there is no danger of a devout believer, overwhelmed by my arguments, being deprived of his faith. Besides, I have said nothing that other and better men have not said before me in a much more complete, forcible and impressive way. The names of these men are well known. I shall not quote them. I should not like to give the impression that I would count myself of their number. I have merely—this is the only thing that is new in my statement—added a certain psychological foundation to the critique of my great predecessors. It is hardly to be expected that just this addition will produce the effect that was denied to the earlier attempts. Certainly I might be asked at this point why I write such things if I am convinced of their ineffectiveness. But we shall come back to that later.

The one person this publication may harm is myself. I shall have to listen to the most unpleasant reproaches on the score of shallowness, narrow-mindedness, and lack of idealism and of understanding for the highest interests of mankind. But on the one hand these remonstrances are not new to me ; and on the other hand, if a man has even in his early years learnt to face the displeasure of his contemporaries, what effect then can it have on him in his old age, when he is certain to be soon beyond the reach of all favour or disfavour ? In former times it was different. Then utterances such as these brought with them a sure foreshortening of one's earthly existence and a speedy approach of the opportunity to gain personal experience of the next life. But, I repeat, those times are over, and to-day such things can be written without endangering even the author ; the most that can happen will be that in this or that country the translation and the circulation of his book will be forbidden—and naturally this will happen just in that country which feels certain of the high standard of its culture. But one must be able to put up with this also, if one makes any plea for wish-renunciation or for acquiescence in fate.

And then it occurred to me to ask whether the

publication of this work might not do some harm
after all—not indeed to a person, but to a cause :
the cause of psycho-analysis. For it cannot be
denied that this is my creation, and that an
abundance of distrust and ill-will has been shown
to it.   If I now come forward with such displeasing
statements, people will be only too ready to dis-
place their feelings from my person on to psycho-
analysis.   Now one can see, it will be said, where
psycho-analysis leads to. The mask is fallen ;
it leads to the denial of God and of an ethical
ideal, as indeed we have always supposed. To
keep us from the discovery, we have been made to
believe that psycho-analysis neither has, nor can
have, a philosophical standpoint.

This pother will be really disagreeable to me
on account of my many fellow-workers, several
of whom do not at all share my attitude to religious
problems. However, psycho-analysis has already
braved many storms, and it must face this new
one also. In reality psycho-analysis is a method
of investigation, an impartial instrument like,
say, the infinitesimal calculus. Even if a physicist
should discover with the help of the latter that
after a certain period the earth will be destroyed,
one would still hesitate to impute destructive
tendencies to the calculus itself, and to proscribe

it on that account. Nothing that I have said
here against the truth-value of religion needed
the support of psycho-analysis; it had been said
by others long before psycho-analysis came into
existence. If one can find a new argument against
the truth of religion by applying the psycho-
analytic method, so much the worse for religion,
but the defenders of religion will with equal right
avail themselves of psycho-analysis in order to
appreciate to the full the affective significance of
religious doctrines.

And now to proceed with the defence : clearly
religion has performed great services for human
culture. It has contributed much toward restraining the asocial instincts, but still not enough.
For many thousands of years it has ruled human
society ; it has had time to show what it can
achieve. If it had succeeded in making happy
the greater part of mankind, in consoling them,
in reconciling them to life, and in making them
into supporters of civilization, then no one would
dream of striving to alter existing conditions.
But instead of this what do we see ? We see
that an appallingly large number of men are dis-
contented with civilization and unhappy in it, and
feel it as a yoke that must be shaken off ; that these
men either do everything in their power to alter

this civilization, or else go so far in their hostility
to it that they will have nothing whatever to do
either with civilization or with restraining their
instincts. At this point it will be objected that
this state of affairs is due to the very fact that
religion has forfeited a part of its influence on
the masses, just because of the deplorable effect
of the advances in science. We shall note this
admission and the reasons given for it, and shall
make use of it later for our own purposes; but
the objection itself has no force.

It is doubtful whether men were in general
happier at a time when religious doctrines held
unlimited sway than they are now; more moral
they certainly were not. They have always
understood how to externalize religious precepts,
thereby frustrating their intentions. And the
priests, who had to enforce religious obedience,
met them half-way. God's kindness must lay a
restraining hand upon his justice. One sinned,
and then one made oblation or did penance, and
then one was free to sin anew. Russian mysticism
has come to the sublime conclusion that sin is
indispensable for the full enjoyment of the blessings
of divine grace, and therefore, fundamentally, it
is pleasing to God. It is well known that the
priests could only keep the masses submissive to

religion by making these great concessions to human instincts. And so it was settled : God alone is strong and good, man is weak and sinful. Immorality, no less than morality, has at all times found support in religion. If the achievements of religion in promoting men's happiness, in adapting them to civilization, and in controlling them morally, are no better, then the question arises whether we are right in considering it necessary for mankind, and whether we do wisely in basing the demands of our culture upon it.

Let us consider the unmistakable character of the present situation. We have heard the admission that religion no longer has the same influence on men that it used to have (we are concerned here with European Christian culture). And this, not because its promises have become smaller, but because they appear less credible to people. Let us admit that the reason—perhaps not the only one—for this change is the increase of the scientific spirit in the higher strata of human society. Criticism has nibbled at the authenticity of religious documents, natural science has shown up the errors contained in them, and the comparative method of research has revealed the fatal resemblance between religious ideas revered by us and the mental productions of primitive ages and peoples.

The scientific spirit engenders a particular attitude to the problems of this world; before the problems of religion it halts for a while, then wavers, and finally here too steps over the threshold. In this process there is no stopping. The more the fruits of knowledge become accessible to men, the more widespread is the decline of religious belief, at first only of the obsolete and objectionable expressions of the same, then of its fundamental assumptions also. The Americans who instituted the monkey trial in Dayton have alone proved consistent. Elsewhere the inevitable transition is accomplished by way of half-measures and insincerities.

Culture has little to fear from the educated or from the brain workers. In their case religious motives for civilized behaviour would be unobtrusively replaced by other and secular ones; besides, for the most part they are themselves supporters of culture. But it is another matter with the great mass of the uneducated and suppressed, who have every reason to be enemies of culture. So long as they do not discover that people no longer believe in God, all is well. But they discover it, infallibly, and would do so even if this work of mine were not published. They are ready to accept the results of scientific thought, without having effected in themselves the process of change which scientific thought induces in men. Is there not a danger that these masses, in their hostility to culture, will attack the weak point which they have discovered in their taskmaster ? If you must not kill your neighbour, solely because God has forbidden it and will sorely avenge it in this or the other life, and you then discover that there is no God so that one need not fear his punishment, then you will certainly kill without hesitation, and you could only be prevented from this by mundane force. And so follows the necessity for either the most rigorous suppression of these dangerous masses and the most careful exclusion of all opportunities for mental awakening, or a fundamental revision of the relation between culture and religion.

E

CHAPTER VIII

O NE would suppose that this last proposal could be carried out without any
special difficulty. It is true that it
would involve some measure of renunciation, but
one would gain, perhaps, more than one lost, and
a great danger would be avoided. But people
have a horror of it, as if civilization would thereby
be exposed to an even greater danger. When
Saint Boniface felled the tree which was venerated
as sacred by the Saxons, those who stood round
expected some fearful event to follow the outrage.
It did not happen, and the Saxons were baptized.

It is manifestly in the interest of man's communal existence, which would not otherwise be
practicable, that civilization has laid down the
commandment that one shall not kill the neighbour whom one hates, who is in one's way, or
whose property one covets. For the murderer
would draw on to himself the vengeance of the
murdered man's kinsmen and the secret envy of

the others who feel as much inward inclination as he did to such an act of violence. Thus he would not enjoy his revenge or his spoil for long, but would have every prospect of being killed soon himself. Even if he could defend himself against single foes by his extraordinary strength and caution, he would be bound to succumb to a combination of these weaker foes. If a combination of this sort did not take place, then murder would continue ceaselessly, and the end of it would be that men would exterminate one another. It would be the same state of affairs among individuals that still prevails in Corsica among families, but otherwise survives only among nations. Insecurity of life, an equal danger for all, now unites men into one society, which forbids the individual to kill and reserves to itself the right to kill in the name of society the man who violates this prohibition. This, then, is justice and punishment.

We do not, however, tell others of this rational basis for the murder prohibition ; we declare, on the contrary, that God is its author. Thus, making bold to divine his intentions, we find that he has no wish, either, for men to exterminate each other. By acting thus we invest the cultural prohibition with a quite peculiar solemnity, but at

the same time we risk making its observance
dependent on belief in God. If we retract this
step, no longer saddling God with our own wishes,
and content ourselves with the social justification
for the cultural prohibition, then we renounce, it
is true, its hallowed nature, but we also avoid
endangering its existence. And we gain something
else as well. Through some kind of diffusion or
infection the character of sanctity and inviola-
bility, of other-worldliness, one might say, has been
extended from some few important prohibitions
to all other cultural institutions and laws and
ordinances. And often the halo becomes these
none too well ; not only do they invalidate each
other by making conflicting decisions according to
the time and place of their origin ; even apart
from this they betray every sign of human in-
adequacy. One can easily recognize among them
things which can only be the product of short-
sightedness and apprehensiveness, the expression
of narrow interests, or the result of inadequate
hypotheses. The criticism to which one must
subject them also diminishes to an unwelcome
extent people's respect for other and more
justified cultural demands. As it is a delicate task
to decide what God has himself ordained and what
derives rather from the authority of an all-

powerful parliament or a supreme judicial decision,
it would be an indubitable advantage to leave
God out of the question altogether, and to admit
honestly the purely human origin of all cultural
laws and institutions.   Along with their preten-
sions to sanctity the rigid and immutable nature
of these laws and regulations would also cease.
Men would realize that these have been made,
not so much to rule them, as, on the contrary, to
serve their interests ; they would acquire a more
friendly attitude to them, and instead of aiming
at their abolition they would aim only at improv-
ing them. This would be an important advance
on the road which leads to reconciliation with the
burden of culture.

But here our plea for a purely rational basis
for cultural laws, that is to say, for deriving them
from social necessity, is interrupted by a sudden
doubt. We have chosen as our example the origin
of the murder prohibition. But does our account
of it correspond to historical truth ? We fear not ;
it appears to be merely a rationalistic construction.
With the help of psycho-analysis we have studied
this very point in the history of human culture,
and supported by this study we are bound to say
that in reality it did not happen like this. Even
in men to-day purely reasonable motives are of

little avail against passionate impulses. How much weaker, then, must they have been in the primordial animal man! Perhaps even now his descendants would still kill one another without inhibition, if there had not been among those acts of murder one—the slaughter of the primal father —which evoked an irresistible emotional reaction, momentous in its consequences. From it arose the commandment: thou shalt not kill, which in totemism was confined to the father-substitute, and was later extended to others, but which even to-day is not universally observed.

But according to arguments which I need not repeat here, that primal father has been the proto-type of God, the model after which later generations have formed their figure of God. Hence the religious explanation is right. God was actually concerned in the origin of that prohibition; his influence, not insight into what was necessary for society, brought it into being. And the process of attributing man's will to God is fully justified; for men, knowing that they had brutally set aside the father, determined, in the reaction to their outrage, to respect his will in future. And so the religious doctrine does give us the historical truth, though of course in a somewhat remodelled and disguised form; our rational explanation belies it.

We now observe that the stock of religious ideas contains not only wish-fulfilments, but also important historical memories. What matchless, what abundant power this combination of past and present must give to religion ! But with the help of an analogy we may perhaps feel our way towards another view of the problem. It is not a good thing to transplant ideas far away from the soil in which they grew, but we cannot resist pointing out the resemblance which forms this analogy. We know that the human child cannot well complete its development towards culture without passing through a more or less distinct phase of neurosis. This is because the child is unable to suppress by rational mental effort so many of those instinctual impulsions which cannot later be turned to account, but has to check them by acts of repression, behind which there stands as a rule an anxiety motive. Most of these child neuroses are overcome spontaneously as one grows up, and especially is this the fate of the obsessional neuroses of childhood. The remainder can be cleared up still later by psycho-analytic treatment. In just the same way one might assume that in its development through the ages mankind as a whole experiences conditions that are analogous to the neuroses, and this for the same reasons, because in the ages of its ignorance and intellectual weakness it achieved by purely affective means the instinctual renunciations, indispensable for man's communal existence. And the residue of these repression-like processes, which took place in antiquity, has long clung on to civilization. Thus religion would be the universal obsessional neurosis of humanity. It, like the child's, originated in the Oedipus complex, the relation to the father. According to this conception one might prophesy that the abandoning of religion must take place with the fateful inexorability of a process of growth, and that we are just now in the middle of this phase of development.

So we should form our behaviour after the model of a sensible teacher, who does not oppose the new development confronting him, but seeks to further it and to temper the force of its onset. To be sure this analogy does not exhaust the essence of religion. If on the one hand religion brings with it obsessional limitations, which can only be compared to an individual obsessional neurosis, it comprises on the other hand a system of wish-illusions, incompatible with reality, such as we find in an isolated form only in Meynert's amentia, a state of blissful hallucinatory confusion.

But these are only just comparisons, with whose help we can endeavour to understand social phenomena ; individual psychology supplies us with no exact counterpart.

It has been shown repeatedly (by myself, and particularly by Theodor Reik) into what details the analogy of religion and the obsessional neurosis may be pursued, how much of the vicissitudes and peculiarities of the formation of religion may be understood in this way. And it accords well with this that the true believer is in a high degree protected against the danger of certain neurotic afflictions ; by accepting the universal neurosis he is spared the task of forming a personal neurosis.

Our knowledge of the historical value of certain religious doctrines increases our respect for them, but it does not invalidate our proposal to exclude them from the motivation of cultural laws. On the contrary ! This historical residue has given us the conception of religious dogmas as, so to speak, neurotic survivals, and now we may say that the time has probably come to replace the consequences of repression by the results of rational mental effort, as in the analytic treatment of neurotics. One may prophesy, but hardly regret, that this process of remodelling will not stop at dispelling the solemn air of sanctity surrounding

the cultural laws, but that a general revision of
these must involve the abolition of many of them.
And this will go far to solve our appointed problem
of reconciling men to civilization. We need not
regret the loss of historical truth involved in
accepting the rational motivation of cultural laws.
The truths contained in religious doctrines are
after all so distorted and systematically disguised
that the mass of mankind cannot recognize them
as truth. It is an instance of the same thing when
we tell the child that new-born babies are brought
by the stork. Here, too, we tell the truth in
symbolic guise, for we know what that large bird
signifies. But the child does not know it ; he hears
only the distortion, and feels that he has been
deceived ; and we know how often his refractori-
ness and his distrust of the grown-ups gets bound
up with this impression. We have come to the
conclusion that it is better to avoid such symbolic
disguisings of the truth, and to allow the child
knowledge of the real state of affairs in a way
suitable for his stage of intellectual development.

CHAPTER IX

You allow yourself contradictions which are hard to reconcile with one another. First you declare that a work like yours is quite harmless ; no one will let himself be robbed of his religious faith through such discussions. But since, as became evident later, it is your aim to disturb this faith, one may ask : why in fact do you publish it ? At another point, however, you admit that it might be dangerous, indeed very dangerous, for a man to discover that people no longer believe in God. Docile though he had been hitherto, now he would throw off all allegiance to the laws of culture. Your whole argument that the religious motivation of the cultural commandments signifies a danger for culture rests, in fact, on the assumption that the believer can be made into an unbeliever. But that is a complete contradiction.

' And here is another contradiction : you admit on the one hand that man will not be guided by intelligence; he is ruled by his passions and by the claims of his instincts; but on the other hand you propose to replace the affective basis of his allegiance to culture by a rational one. Let who can understand this. To me it seems a case of either the one or the other.

'Besides, have you learnt nothing from history? Once before such an attempt to substitute reason for religion was made, officially and in the grand manner. Surely you remember the French Revolution and Robespierre, and also how short-lived and how deplorably ineffectual the experiment? It is being repeated in Russia at present, and we need not be curious about the result. Do you not think we may assume that man cannot do without religion?

'You have said yourself that religion is more than an obsessional neurosis. But you have not dealt with this other aspect of it. You are content to work out the analogy with the neurosis. Men must be freed from a neurosis. What else is lost in the process does not trouble you.'

Probably these apparent contradictions have arisen because I have been dealing too hastily with complicated matters, but we can make up for this to some extent. I still maintain that in one respect my work is quite harmless. No believer will let himself be led astray by these or by similar arguments. A believer has certain ties of affection binding him to the substance of religion. There are certainly a vast number of other people who are not religious in the same sense. They obey the laws of civilization because they are intimidated by the threats of religion, and they fear religion so long as they consider it as a part of the reality that restricts them. These are the people who break free as soon as they dare to give up their belief in its reality value ; but arguments have no effect on them either. They cease to fear religion when they find that others do not fear it, and of these I have asserted that they would learn of the decline of religious influence even if I did not publish my work.

But I suppose you yourself attach more value to the other contradiction with which you tax me. Since men are so slightly amenable to reasonable arguments, so completely are they ruled by their instinctual wishes, why should one want to take away from them a means of satisfying their instincts and replace it by reasonable arguments ? Certainly men are like this, but have you asked yourself whether they need be so, whether their inmost nature necessitates it ? Can an anthropologist give the cranial index of a people whose custom it is to deform their children's heads by bandaging them from their earliest years ? Think of the distressing contrast between the radiant intelligence of a healthy child and the feeble mentality of the average adult. Is it so utterly impossible that it is just religious up-bringing which is largely to blame for this relative degeneration ? I think it would be a very long time before a child who was not influenced began to trouble himself about God and the things beyond this world. Perhaps his thoughts on these matters would then take the same course as they did with his ancestors ; but we do not wait for this development ; we introduce him to the doctrines of religion at a time when he is neither interested in them nor capable of grasping their import Is it not true that the two main points in the modern educational programme are the retardation of sexual development and the early application of religious influence ? So when the child's mind awakens, the doctrines of religion are already unassailable. But do you suppose that it is particularly conducive to the strengthening of the mental function that so important a sphere should be closed to it by the menace of hell pains ? We need not be greatly surprised at the feeble mentality of the man who has once brought himself to accept without criticism all the absurdities that religious doctrines repeat to him, and even to overlook the contradictions between them. Now we have no other means of controlling our instincts than our intelligence. And how can we expect people who are dominated by thought-prohibitions to attain the psychological ideal, the primacy of the intelligence? You know too that women in general are said to suffer from so-called ' physiological weak-mindedness ', *i.e.* a poorer intelligence than the man's. The fact itself is disputable, its interpretation doubtful; but it has been argued for the secondary nature of this intellectual degeneration that women labour under the harshness of the early prohibition, which prevented them from applying their mind to what would have interested them most, that is to say, to the problems of sexual life. So long as a man's early years are influenced by the religious thought-inhibition and by the loyal one derived from it, as well as by the sexual one, we cannot really say what he is actually like.

But I will curb my ardour and admit the possibility that I too am chasing after an illusion. Perhaps the effect of the religious thought-prohibition is not as bad as I assume, perhaps it will

turn out that human nature remains the same
even if education is not abused by being subjected
to religion.   I do not know, and you cannot know
either.   It is not only the great problems of this
life that seem at present insoluble ; there are many
smaller questions also that are hard to decide.
But you must admit that there is here the justification for a hope for the future, that perhaps we
may dig up a treasure which can enrich culture,
and that it is worth while to make the experiment of a non-religious education.   Should it
prove unsatisfactory, I am ready to give up the
reform and to return to the earlier, purely descriptive judgement : man is a creature of weak
intelligence who is governed by his instinctual
wishes.

There is another point in which I whole-
heartedly agree with you.   It is, to be sure, a
senseless proceeding to try and do away with
religion by force and at one blow—more especially
as it is a hopeless one.   The believer will not let
his faith be taken from him, neither by arguments
nor by prohibitions.   And even if it did succeed
with some, it would be a cruel thing to do.   A
man who has for decades taken a sleeping
draught is naturally unable to sleep if he is deprived of it.   That the effect of the consolations

of religion may be compared to that of a narcotic
is prettily illustrated by what is happening in
America. There they are now trying—plainly
under the influence of petticoat government—
to deprive men of all stimulants, intoxicants and
luxuries,[1] and to satiate them with piety by
way of compensation. This is another experiment about .the result of which we need not be
curious.

And so I disagree with you when you go on to
argue that man cannot in general do without the
consolation of the religious illusion, that without
it he would not endure the troubles of life, the
cruelty of reality. Certainly this is true of the
man into whom you have instilled the sweet—or
bitter-sweet—poison from childhood on. But what
of the other, who has been brought up soberly?
Perhaps he, not suffering from neurosis, will need
no intoxicant to deaden it. True, man will then
find himself in a difficult situation. He will have
to confess his utter helplessness and his insignificant
part in the working of the universe; he will have
to confess that he is no longer the centre of creation,
no longer the object of the tender care of a benevolent providence. He will be in the same
position as the child who has left the home where

[1] *I.e.* tea, alcohol, and tobacco.

F

he was so warm and comfortable. But, after all, is it not the destiny of childishness to be overcome? Man cannot remain a child for ever; he must venture at last into the hostile world. This may be called 'education to reality'; need I tell you that it is the sole aim of my book to draw attention to the necessity for this advance?

You fear, probably, that he will not stand the test? Well, anyhow, let us be hopeful. It is at least something to know that one is thrown on one's own resources. One learns then to use them properly. And man is not entirely without means of assistance; since the time of the deluge science has taught him much, and it will still further increase his power. And as for the great necessities of fate, against which there is no remedy, these he will simply learn to endure with resignation. Of what use to him is the illusion of a kingdom on the moon, whose revenues have never yet been seen by anyone? As an honest crofter on this earth he will know how to cultivate his plot in a way that will support him. Thus by withdrawing his expectations from the other world and concentrating all his liberated energies on this earthly life he will probably attain to a state of things in which life will be tolerable for all and no one will be oppressed by culture any more. Then with one of our comrades in unbelief he will be able to say without regret :

> Let us leave the heavens
> To the angels and the sparrows.

CHAPTER X

THAT does sound splendid. A race of men that has renounced all illusions and has thus become capable of making its existence on the earth a tolerable one! But I cannot share your expectations. And this, not because I am the pig-headed reactionary you perhaps take me for. No; it is because I am a sensible person. It seems to me that we have now exchanged rôles; you prove to be the enthusiast, who allows himself to be carried away by illusions, and I represent the claims of reason, the right to be sceptical. What you have just stated seems to me to be founded on errors, which after your precedent I may call illusions because they betray clearly enough the influence of your wishes. You indulge in the hope that generations which have not experienced the influence of religious teaching in early childhood will easily attain the wished-for primacy of the intelligence over the life of the instincts. That is surely an illusion; in this decisive point human nature is hardly likely to alter. If I am not mistaken—one knows so little of other civilizations —there are even to-day peoples who do not grow up under the pressure of a religious system, and they come no nearer your ideal than the others. If you wish to expel religion from our European civilization you can only do it through another system of doctrines, and from the outset this would take over all the psychological characteristics of religion, the same sanctity, rigidity and intolerance, the same prohibition of thought in self-defence.   Something of this sort you must have in justice to the requirements of education.   For you cannot do without education.   The way from sucking child to civilized man is a long one ; too many young people would go astray and fail to arrive at their life tasks in due time if they were left without guidance to their own development. The doctrines made use of in their education will always confine the thought of their riper years, exactly as you reproach religion with doing to-day. Do you not observe that it is the ineradicable natural defect of our, of every, culture that it imposes on the child, governed by his instincts and intellectually weak, the making of decisions to which only the matured intelligence of the grown-up can do justice ?   But owing to the fact

that mankind's development through the ages
is concentrated into a few years of childhood
culture cannot do otherwise, and it is only by
affective influence that the child can be induced
to accomplish the task assigned to it. And so
this is the outlook for your " primacy of the
intellect ".

' And now you should not be surprised if I
intervene on behalf of retaining the religious
system of teaching as the basis of education and
of man's communal life. It is a practical problem,
not a question of reality value. Since we cannot,
for the sake of the preservation of our culture,
postpone influencing the individual until he has
become ready for culture—many would never be
so anyhow—and since we are obliged to press some
system of teaching on the growing child which
shall have the effect on him of a postulate that
does not admit of criticism, it seems to me that
the religious system is by far the most suitable
for the purpose ; of course just on account of that
quality—its power for wish-fulfilment and consolation—by which you claim to have recognized
it as an " illusion ". In face of the difficulty of
discovering anything about reality, indeed the
doubt whether this is possible for us at all, we
must not overlook the fact that human needs

are also a part, and indeed an important part, of reality, and one that concerns us particularly closely.

' I find another advantage of religious doctrine in one of its peculiarities, to which you seem to take particular exception. It admits of an ideational refinement and sublimation, by which it can be divested of most of those traces of a primitive and infantile way of thinking which it bears. What is then left is a body of ideas which science no longer contradicts and which it cannot disprove. These modifications of religious doctrine, which you have condemned as half-measures and compromises, make it possible to bridge the gap between the uneducated masses and the philosophical thinker, and to preserve that common bond between them which is so important for the protection of culture. With it you would have no need to fear that the poor man would discover that the upper strata of society " no longer believe in God ". I think I have shown by now that your endeavour reduces itself to the attempt to replace a proved and affectively valuable illusion by one that is unproved and without affective value.'

You shall not find me impervious to your criticism. I know how difficult it is to avoid illusions ; perhaps even the hopes I have confessed to are of an illusory nature. But I hold fast to one distinction. My illusions—apart from the fact that no penalty is imposed for not sharing them—are not, like the religious ones, incapable of correction, they have no delusional character. If experience should show—not to me, but to others after me who think as I do—that we are mistaken, then we shall give up our expectations. Take my endeavour for what it is. A psychologist, who does not deceive himself about the difficulty of finding his bearings in this world, strives to review the development of mankind in accord with what insight he has won from studying the mental processes of the individual during his development from childhood to manhood. In this connection the idea forces itself upon him that religion is comparable to a childhood neurosis, and he is optimistic enough to assume that mankind will overcome this neurotic phase, just as so many children grow out of their similar neuroses. These pieces of knowledge from individual psychology may be inadequate, their application to the human race unjustified, the optimism without foundation ; I grant you the uncertainty of all these things. But often we cannot refrain from saying what we think, excusing ourselves on the ground that it is given for no more than it is worth.

And there are two points that I must dwell on a little longer. First, the weakness of my position does not betoken any strengthening of yours. I think you are defending a lost cause. We may insist as much as we like that the human intellect is weak in comparison with human instincts, and be right in doing so. But nevertheless there is something peculiar about this weakness. The voice of the intellect is a soft one, but it does not rest until it has gained a hearing. Ultimately, after endlessly repeated rebuffs, it succeeds. This is one of the few points in which one may be optimistic about the future of mankind, but in itself it signifies not a little. And one can make it a starting-point for yet other hopes. The primacy of the intellect certainly lies in the far, far, but still probably not infinite, distance. And as it will presumably set itself the same aims that you expect to be realized by your God—of course within human limits, in so far as external reality, 'Ανάγκη, allows it—the brotherhood of man and the reduction of suffering, we may say that our antagonism is only a temporary and not an irreconcilable one. We desire the same things, but you are more impatient, more exacting, and—why should I not say it—more selfish than I and those like me. You would have the state of bliss to begin immediately after death; you ask of it the impossible, and you will not surrender the claim of the individual. Of these wishes our god Λόγος [1] will realize those which external nature permits, but he will do this very gradually, only in the incalculable future and for other children of men. Compensation for us, who suffer grievously from life, he does not promise. On the way to this distant goal your religious doctrines will have to be discarded, no matter whether the first attempts fail, or whether the first substitute-formations prove to be unstable. You know why; in the long run nothing can withstand reason and experience, and the contradiction religion offers to both is only too palpable. Not even the purified religious ideas can escape this fate, so long as they still try to preserve anything of the consolation of religion. Certainly if you confine yourself to the belief in a higher spiritual being, whose qualities are indefinable and whose intentions cannot be discerned, then you are proof against the interference of science, but then you will also relinquish the interest of men.

And secondly: note the difference between

[1] The twin gods Λόγος-'Ανάγκη of the Dutchman *Multatuli*.

your attitude to illusions and mine. You have
to defend the religious illusion with all your might ;
if it were discredited—and to be sure it is sufficiently
menaced—then your world would collapse, there
would be nothing left for you but to despair of
everything, of culture and of the future of mankind.
From this bondage I am, we are, free. Since we
are prepared to renounce a good part of our
infantile wishes, we can bear it if some of our
expectations prove to be illusions.

Education freed from the burden of religious
doctrines will not perhaps effect much alteration
in man's psychological nature ; our god Λόγος is
not perhaps a very powerful one ; he may only
fulfil a small part of what his forerunners have
promised. If we have to acknowledge this, we
shall do so with resignation. We shall not thereby
lose our interest in the world and in life, for we
have in one respect a sure support which you lack.
We believe that it is possible for scientific work
to discover something about the reality of the
world through which we can increase our power
and according to which we can regulate our life.
If this belief is an illusion, then we are in the
same position as you, but science has shown us by
numerous and significant successes that it is no
illusion. Science has many open, and still more

secret, enemies among those who cannot forgive
it for having weakened religious belief and for
threatening to overthrow it. People reproach it
for the small amount it has taught us and the
incomparably greater amount it has left in the
dark. But then they forget how young it is,
how difficult its beginnings, and how infinitesi-
mally small the space of time since the human
intellect has been strong enough for the tasks it
sets it. Do we not all do wrong in that the
periods of time which we make the basis of our
judgements are of too short duration ? We should
take an example from the geologist. People com-
plain of the unreliability of science, that she
proclaims as a law to-day what the next generation
will recognize to be an error and which it will
replace by a new law of equally short currency.
But that is unjust and in part untrue. The transformation of scientific ideas is a process of development and progress, not of revolution. A law that
was at first held to be universally valid proves
to be a special case of a more comprehensive law,
or else its scope is limited by another law not
discovered until later ; a rough approximation
to the truth is replaced by one more carefully
adjusted, which in its turn awaits a further approach
to perfection. In several spheres we have not

yet surmounted a phase of investigation in which
we test hypotheses that have soon to be rejected
as inadequate ; but in others we have already an
assured and almost immutable core of knowledge.
Finally an attempt has been made to discredit
radically scientific endeavour on the ground that,
bound as it is to the conditions of our own organization, it can yield nothing but subjective results,
while the real nature of things outside us remains
inaccessible to it.   But this is to disregard several
factors of decisive importance for the understanding
of scientific work.   Firstly, our organization, *i.e.*
our mental apparatus, has been developed actually
in the attempt to explore the outer world, and
therefore it must have realized in its structure a
certain measure of appropriateness ;   secondly,
it itself is a constituent part of that world
which we are to investigate, and readily admits
of such investigation ; thirdly, the task of science
is fully circumscribed if we confine it to showing
how the world must appear to us in consequence
of the particular character of our organization ;
fourthly, the ultimate findings of science, just
because of the way in which they are attained,
are conditioned not only by our organization
but also by that which has affected this organization ; and, finally, the problem of the nature

of the world irrespective of our perceptive mental apparatus is an empty abstraction without practical interest.

No, science is no illusion. But it would be an illusion to suppose that we could get anywhere else what it cannot give us.